For Alexis and Daniel,
The Answers to My Prayers

If I Pray to God for Chocolate, Will He Answer...?

by

Marion Witherspoon Bankhead

If I Pray for Chocolate, Will He Answer?
1st Edition

Published by W.E. Power Collaborative
      P.O. Box 667088
      Houston, Texas 77266
      w.e.powercollaborative7@gmail.com

Text Copyright © Marion Witherspoon Bankhead, 2013
Illustration Copyright © Can Stock Photo, Inc., 2011, 2012
All rights reserved. Accept as permitted under the U.S. Copyright Act of 1976, No part of this publication may be reproduced, distributed or transmitted in any form or by any means, or stored in a database or retrieval system, without the prior written permission of the publisher and author.

Library of Congress Control Number 2016916759
ISBN 9780692786543

Printed in the United States of America

Scripture taken from the New International Version of the Bible

Today is a great day because I learned something new!

I learned something new that anyone can do. My mom told me while she pushed me on my swing,

That God's love is so big that I can pray for anything!

I can pray when playing ball and I'm afraid I'll miss the net. I can ask God to help me and I know He'll say "don't fret!"

And even when I pray to God and He does not say yes,

I'm honestly okay with it, 'cause I know
His will is best!

I can pray there will be people at my lemonade stand - a huge crowd, a stampede, a parade and a band!

I can pray that thirsty people who are out for a jog will stop for a drink, for themselves or their dog.

I can pray at the toy store, at the candy store or mall, and I can still be thankful if I get nothing at all.

I can pray when it's my dad's turn to bake the classroom cake. I will close my eyes real tightly and recite **Philippians 4:8**, so I'll think only good things. That means I won't be nervous when dad makes the icing.

⁸ Finally, brothers and sisters, whatever is true, whatever is noble, whatever is right, whatever is pure, whatever is lovely, whatever is admirable—if anything is excellent or praiseworthy—think about such things.

I can pray and say thanks when I feel God's love in my heart. That is His way of telling me we are never apart.

We are never apart—no matter how far I travel…on a plane, on a train or to my driveway gravel.

And even when I fall over
In my favorite cardboard box,
He is right there showing me
how to handle life's hard
knocks.

I can pray while in the sandbox,
I can pray while on the swing...

I thank God I can pray when it comes to bullying.

I can pray for the bullies, that's what I can do. I can pray that the bullies will learn to pray, too. I can pray that the bullies will find perfect peace and that the sadness they feel will soon be released.

I can pray as I fight sleep with every bit of my might. I can pray as I realize I'm all out of fight.

My eyelids are suddenly heavier than steel, with my head toward the heavens, on my knees I will kneel...

On my knees I will kneel as I pray to my Savior and I thank Him for his love no matter what my behavior.

I thank God for the awesome plans He has prepared for me, and I pray His plans include something really

Chocolatey...

But my steps are ordered by the Lord you see, as it is written in Psalms 37:23 ...

> ²³ The Lord makes firm the steps of one who delights in him.

I thank God for the honor of praying to Him, whether it's for chocolate, toys, or a puppy that swims.

I thank Him for his mercy, his kindness and care. I thank Him for the love He gives to children everywhere.

So even when you pray to God for chocolate and He does not say yes, don't forget to say thank you Lord, 'cause we know

His will is best!

Amen!

www.ingramcontent.com/pod-product-compliance
Lightning Source LLC
Chambersburg PA
CBHW041234040426
42444CB00002B/153